Read To Me My Love

A Ballad about Being Together

By Rhea Wessel

Illustrations by Pascal Thomas

mywunderkind.com Publishing

mywunderkind.com Publishing

Rhea Wessel
Schreyerstr. 57 • 61476 Kronberg im Taunus • Germany

ISBN-13: 978-0-9970625-1-9

To Isabella, with love

My mother takes a deep breath.

She wants to say something.

I set the book down and move
my ear close to her mouth.

She whispers: "Read to me, my love."

I return to the book, glancing between
the lines to watch her breathe.

Chest rising, chest falling.

Hope rising, hope falling.

My mom always read to me
when I was small.

Even before I was born,
she rested the book on her
protruding stomach.

• • •

She read aloud,
waiting for me
to *kick* and say,

"When you read to me,
time stands still
You give to me what is my fill
I have you there
for me alone
Freed from modern thief, smart-phone."

While she nursed me,
mom read.
Voraciously.

A book about women.
Freeing themselves.

Living lives where they decide.

At the good parts, she'd say,

"Hey baby, remember this."

• • •

She read aloud,
waiting for me
to *bite* and say,

"When you read to me,
time stands still
You give to me what is my fill
I have you there
for me alone
Freed from modern thief, smart-phone."

I grew and grew and toddled
to the reading chair.

Each night a rite into
the world of dreams.

Arriving there on
the wings of words.

I became the characters
I met in mom's books –

weaklings, stronglings,
heroes and rebels.

School started, friends called
and time slipped away.

I was too old for mom's lap
and the reading chair.

But when I got sick,
when I was feeling down,
mom, my wonderful mom, she read aloud.

• • •

Reading time became healing time.

Time to think.
Time to dream.
Time to be.

I learned to pick myself up.
To face my fears.

I found the courage to change my life.

As I lived and loved,
I drew on characters
only known in my imagination.

And when love was lost,
when I stumbled and cried,

Characters stronger than me
gave me guts.

Those weaker than me
kept my feet on the ground.

Then one day I met my mate.

I knew it was him
when

• • •

He read aloud,
waiting for me
to *kiss* and say,

"When you read to me,
time stands still
You give to me what is my fill
I have you there
for me alone
Freed from modern thief, smart-phone."

Our baby was born,
a little girl.

Writing her life.

Hungry for words.

At grandma's bedside,
that baby turns to me to say,

"Mom, why do you read
when grandma can't hear?"

I read aloud, *wanting* for
grandma to kick and say,

"When you read to me,
time stands still
You give to me what is my fill
I have you there for me alone
Freed from modern thief, smart-phone."

• • •

With that we watch as grandma sleeps.
Drifting into the world of night stories.

We hold each other, rocking to and fro.
We touch grandma's hands.
We comb her hair.

With sorrow, we grab the book.
The same book grandma read to me.
The same book I read to you, my child.

Grandma sleeps tonight,
email forever unread.

She is free.

Finally free.

I turn to her
in a whisper and say,

"Dear mom,
You knew how to make
time stand still.

You knew how to give me life's fill.

I hope you know that
in that time we had alone,

You gave the gift of story –

and taught me how to hold my own."

www.ingramcontent.com/pod-product-compliance
Lightning Source LLC
Chambersburg PA
CBHW041245040426
42445CB00005B/149